STORIES OF MUKUNDA

EARLY LIFE OF
PARAMAHANSA YOGANANDA

SPI Publications

Published by SPI Publications, www.spipublications.in
SPI, the SPI logo, and Split Poetry India are trademarks of SPI Publications, or its affiliates.
ISBN-13: 978-93-49860-17-9

First Edition 2025

SPI Publications

Corporate & Editorial Office

117/2, Sector 37, Khandsa Road,
Gurgaon, Haryana 122 001
Phone: +91 98355 52940
Email: contact@spipublications.in
Website: www.spipublications.in

Processed and Printed in India

STORIES OF MUKUNDA

EARLY LIFE OF PARAMAHANSA YOGANANDA

FOREWORD

This book is an early collection of reminiscences of wisdom and wit of the great Kriya Yoga Master Paramahansa Yogananda. The book was previously published by Self Realization Fellowship, written by Swami Kriyanandaji in the year 1958. He left the organization in the year 1962 and the copyright was not renewed by SRF, in the year 1978. (When it was needed to renew.)

Hence copyright of this book is expired, after its first publication in the year 1958, plus 36 years, that is in the year 1994. (As per the U.S.A. Copyright law.) Therefore, we can conclude that this book is in the Public Domain, as per the U.S.A. and Indian Copyright Act.

The said book was out of publication since long back, and now after 65 years of its first publication, the editor is happy to make this wonderful book available once again to a world-wide audience.

A Yogi in Death as in Life

Paramahansa Yogananda entered mahasamadhi (a yogi's final conscious exit from the body) in Los Angeles, California, US.A. on March 7, 1952, after concluding his speech at a banquet held in honor of H.E. Binay R. Sen, Ambassador of India. The story of the beloved yogi's passing was reported in Self-Realization Magazine (Los Angeles), May 1952 issue; and in the national news weekly Time, August 4, 1952 issue.

The great world teacher demonstrated the value of yoga (scientific techniques for God-realization) not only in life but in death. Weeks after his departure his unchanged face shone with the divine luster of incorruptibility.

Mr. Barry T. Rowe, Los Angeles Mortuary Director, Forest Lawn Memorial-Park (in which the body of the great master is temporarily placed), sent Self-Realization Fellowship a notarized letter from which the following extracts are taken:

"The absence of any visual signs of decay in the dead body of Paramahansa Yogananda offers the most extraordinary case in our experience . . . . No physical disintegration was visible in his body even twenty days after death . . . . No indication of mold was visible on his skin, and no visible desiccation (drying up) took place in the bodily tissues. This state of perfect preservation of a body is, so far as we know from mortuary annals, an unparalleled one . . . . At the time of receiving Yogananda's body, the Mortuary personnel expected to observe, through the glass lid of the casket, the usual progressive signs of bodily decay. Our astonishment increased as day followed day without bringing any visible change in the body under observation. Yogananda's body was apparently in a phenomenal state of immutability . . . . No odor of decay emanated from his body at any time . . . . The physical appearance of Yogananda on March 27th, just before the bronze cover of the casket was put into position, was the same as it had been on March 7th.

He looked on March 27th as fresh and as unravaged by decay as he looked on the night of his death. On March 27th there was no reason to say that his body had suffered any visible physical disintegration at all."

Paramhansa Yogananda was born as Mukund Lal Ghosh (also known as Swami Yogananda) in a Bengali Hindu family on January 5, 1893 in Gorakhpur, India. He showed signs of spiritual awareness even as a young child. His quest to find a great Guru to guide him in his spiritual path led him to Swami Sri Yukteswar Giri, who molded the young man who was to become a great spiritual force. After his college graduation in 1915, he took formal vows and was from that time on called Swami Yogananda Giri. Then in 1935, when he returned to India to visit his Guru, Swami Sri Yukteswar Giri bestowed upon him the title of "Paramhansa." The "supreme swan," of which this title is named after, is a mythological bird that can separate water from milk and drink the milk.

He was the first yoga master of India to permanently live and teach in the West. Yogananda arrived in America in 1920, and travelled throughout the United States on what he called his 'spiritual campaigns' to teach the Science of Kriya Yoga.

Yoganandaji taught Kriya yoga, an ancient yoga system, to his followers, which He called the 'Jet-Airplane' route to God. Kriya yoga is an advanced pranayama technique, which revitalizes the life force in the brain and spine. Practicing Kriya yoga elevates the state of mind to achieve spiritual goals and feel oneness with Universe. He continued to lecture and write up-to his passing (Maha-Samadhi) in 1952

His book **"Autobiography of a Yogi"** has been in print for the last seventy years and has been translated into over forty languages. It has been highly acclaimed as a spiritual classic and is designated as one of the 100 Most Important Spiritual Books of the 20th Century.

STORIES OF MUKUNDA

Fourteen anecdotes of the early life of Mukunda Lal Ghosh, humble devotee of God, later known to the world under his monastic name of Paramahansa Yogananda.

By

BROTHER KRIYANANDA

PREFACE

These are true stories. The fourteen anecdotes are among those that Paramahansa Yogananda recounted to lecture audiences in America or that were told to SRF disciples by his relatives and friends who had known him in his early life in India.

In his narratives the great Master did not always mention names, dates, and places. He would often start out: “One time, this friend and I...” and then proceed with the tale. Therefore, in writing the stories, I have not always been certain about the chronology, settings, and personal names. I have found it expedient to bestow fictitious names on certain people in various episodes. The only true names are Mukunda, Sri Yukteswarji, Ananta, Roma, Prabhas Chandra Ghose, and “Maid-Ma.”

To increase narrative interest, in a few instances I have included in one story two or more incidents that in actuality were not closely connected in time.

I am grateful to several disciples at SRF headquarters who edited the manuscript, read the proof sheets, and supplied me with additional factual details,

During Paramahansaji’s last years I had the blessing, as a disciple at Mount Washington Center, of seeing the Master often.

In this book I have tried to depict in words, which are inadequate at best, the spirit of Yoganandaji: a spirit ardent with love for God, tender with sympathy for all men, forgiving, kindly, humorous; yet resolute and forceful when strength was needed; never afraid to side with a righteous cause, however unpopular.

What wonder that the Master's message of man's divinity was blazoned across the earth even during his lifetime? Or that thousands heard and answered it, changing their lives with a newborn faith to conform to the ideals set before them by the compassionate Guru?

BROTHER KRIYANANDA
(formerly Donald Walters)
Minister,

Self-Realization Fellowship Church

Los Angeles, California
December 16, 1953

STORIES OF MUKUNDA

STORIES OF MUKUNDA

A LETTER TO GOD

Mukunda felt such tenderness when he thought of God! Everything that he did or thought he longed to share with his Heavenly Father. Once, when he was a very little boy, he wrote, in the Bengali language, a letter to God. There he poured out everything that he wanted to say to Him. He addressed the letter, "God in Heaven," and mailed it trustingly.

After two or three days he began looking for a reply. Each day letters came—for his father, his mother, even for his elder brother, but—no letter for Mukunda.

"Surely the Lord must have had time to answer by now," Mukunda thought anxiously. "Can't He spare just a few minutes to write me?" Every day the little boy waited eagerly for the postman. Alas! no letter came.

"Dear God," he prayed lovingly, "You must answer my letter. I said so many things to You—so many important things!"

Weeks passed; his longing never abated.

Finally one day he saw a great light. In that light, to his indescribable joy, every part of his letter was answered—and in Bengali script!t

God had answered at last the letter of the child who had refused to give up a loving expectation.

THE GOLDFISH TRAGEDY

Once, when Mukunda was six years old, he brought home a goldfish given to him by his aunt. The fish was put in a tank where water was stored for domestic purposes such as cleaning and scouring. One of the first things Mukunda did every morning was to go to the tank to watch the pretty whirlings of the fish. In this daily visit he was usually joined by his elder brother Ananta and his eldest sister Roma.

One morning Roma was the first to get up. She went as usual to gaze into the tank. The fish was missing! Looking around, she was horrified to find it lying dead on the cement floor a short distance from the tank.

"Who killed the little goldfish?" she cried.

A servant confessed that he had hastily taken water from the tank for his housework and had inadvertently lifted out the fish in the bucket he was using. In splashing the water on the floor, he had caused the death of the fish.

Mukunda soon appeared on the scene. When he saw what had happened, he cried, "My little fish! My poor little fish!" Alternately he wept for the goldfish and stormed at the servant who had killed it.

Unpacified by anything said by his relatives, Mukunda left the scene of one of the first tragedies in his life and climbed the stairs to the highest floor. There his sobs continued. He would not look at his Bengali and English primers nor touch any food that morning.

His father understood the child's grief. A strict disciplinarian, he told the servant that there could be no room in his home for such a careless worker, But the dismissal was no consolation to Mukunda. What, alas, could replace his little goldfish?

His father had to go to the office; his elder brother departed for school. The mother and sister were faced with the problem of comforting Mukunda.

Seeing her child fasting, the mother would take no food herself. She asked his sister to try once more to talk with him. Mukunda was hiding himself.

Roma searched until she found him sitting on the topmost stair, his face darkened with sorrow, his eyes still wet with tears.

Soothingly his sister reasoned with him. He appeared not to hear her. But when she explained that their mother also was fasting, because of him, he yielded."

Roma lifted him in her arms to carry him downstairs. As she did so, she discovered that both his hands were tightly closed.

"What are you hiding, little brother?" she asked softly.

"Please, don't ask me," Mukunda replied.

"Do just let me see, won't you?"

"No, no, please don't," he implored her, hiding his little fists from her gaze.

But at last he reluctantly agreed to reveal his secret.

When he opened his hands, she saw that in one of them he had a small pencil.

In the other hand he held a tiny diary. On a page he had written in English:

my red fish is die

Mukunda, whose later poems were to thrill the soul of the world, had struggled for the first time with words, in memory of one of God's creatures.

THE LIVING KALI*

The heart of youthful Mukunda danced in harmony with God's creation. By day, as he walked around, his mind was fixed firmly at the point between the eyebrows, the seat of the divine or "single" eye.

By night, while others slept, he invoked the Divine Presence. Often, when his father would find him meditating late at night and would put food by his door, Mukunda would give the meal to his dog. Was not God, Mukunda thought, his sufficient sustenance? He realized that he needed to give but little care to his body and its needs.

His elder brother, Ananta, scoffed at him. "Your life will become like dry leaves," he said one day, "of no use to anyone."

Mukunda smiled gaily and retorted, "Perhaps. But dry leaves, dear brother, fertilize the earth."

*Goddess Kali is a symbol of God in the aspect of the Divine Mother. Paramahansaji wrote: "That aspect of the Uncreated Infinite which is active in creation is referred to in Hindu scriptures as the Divine Mother. It is this personalized aspect of the Absolute that may be said to have 'longings' for the rightful behavior of Her children and to answer their prayers.

Men who imagine that the Impersonal cannot manifest in a personal form are in effect denying Its omnipotence and the possibility that man can commune with his Maker.

The Lord in the form of the Cosmic Mother appears in living tangibility before true bhaktas (devotees of a Personal God)."

Whenever he found a sympathetic ear he would speak of his love for the Divine Mother—Her beauty, Her tenderness, Her power to banish the night of maya that veils the soul. His little friends would listen, enthralled. Inflamed by his divine devotion they, too, sought Kali's love.

Out into the quiet woods the small group often went, or for strolls by the 'Ganges, or for service to Kali among the poor. Sometimes they played children's games, and laughed, and sang; but in their romps they had an unseen Playmate, ever included in their fun— Kali. And then the wavelets would dance along the riverbank; the fish would slither and splash about with merriment; the leaves would flutter in frolic on the branches of the trees; the wind would sing sportive measures through the meadow grass: all Nature would play with them, who played with Kali.

One day Mukunda and his friends were walking home just after sunset. Gray-clad shadows, night's tender emissaries, crowded the western skies. It was time for supper. Homes were fragrant with the odors of evening meals; gay sounds streamed from open windows and patios. Mukunda and the other boys smiled softly; Kali, their Mother, was dressing Bengal for the night.

A young friend approached the group. His eyes were shining. He brought what he knew was good news.

"Mukunda," he cried, "and all of you—Listen! I have found a temple—one we haven't seen before. My brother took me to it today. It's a temple of Kali."

"Kali! Kali!" Mukunda's 'companions exclaimed. "Let us go tonight."

Kali, in image or in reality, Kali it was that they loved. Mukunda, who had taught them to feel this love, would no doubt be the first among them to want to visit the newly found temple.

But Mukunda's mood was withdrawn. “You go,” he said. “I 'll stay home tonight.”

“Stay home! But why?” His friends simply couldn't understand him. Hadn't he just sung to them of Kali in the fields? Hadn't he just talked to them of Kali in the town? Would he neglect Kali in the temple, and go home to bed? Impossible, they thought. Yet, their continued pleas failed to move Mukunda. Smiling as though to himself, he left the little group.

His friends went on to the temple without him. There they prostrated themselves in front of the image of Kali. They prayed and sang before Her, and then sat in meditation. The temporary peace that accompanies religious rites humbly performed stole over them.

At home, Mukunda went to his room. He sat to worship the Kali that resides in the temple of the "soul, Of what use to him were outer images?

Mother Night, in whose cradle of sleep the day's trials are banished, now spoke softly to Bengal. Her voice was in the wind, in the twinkling stars. She spoke caressingly, soothing away all human cares. Through the long day men had labored. Now they could lay their burdens on her lap of oblivion.

But sleep was far from Mukunda that night. With ever growing yearning he called to the Divine Mother to come.

“Mother with lotus feet!” he cried. “Mother with dark hair flowing over creation! Mother with the light of laughter in Your eyes!

Your child is calling You, a little child that longs for Your love. Mother Divine! Will You come? Tear asunder this veil that hides You from me!"

The room was tranquil with the stillness of his mind, with the fixity of his devotion. As the clouds sometimes drift in bright transparency around the moon, enhancing her loveliness, so a cloudlike peace stole over Mukunda's soul; he knew that his Divine Mother was not far away.

Chanting Her name, suddenly he saw Her form! Fairer it was than moonbeams on a lotus. In Her hair the stars shone like diamonds. Over the pathway of infinity She danced—lightly, rhythmically—dispelling creation's mood of darkness from before Mukunda's enraptured gaze. Her love seemed to shatter his heart into a million ecstatic fragments.

"Kali!" he whispered, "Mother Kali, You have come!-Destroy forever all Your child's delusion! Keep him ever near You! How beautiful You are! O Mother, may I never forget You, not even for an instant!"

The Divine Mother smiled. "You never will, my child. You may cross the seas, mix with men of other lands, and hear strange tongues—but in your heart of hearts you will be ever in My formless presence. And whenever you call Me, in this form I shall come to you."

A DOUBLE VICTORY

Mukunda attended for some time a school in which a certain boy took pleasure in attacking the younger children. One day, as the bully was inflicting on tiny Bharatam a brutal beating, Mukunda felt a surge of righteous, anger.

Striding up to the bully, who was spill twice his size, Mukunda told him to leave Bharatam alone. "If you want to fight," Mukunda said, "then fight with me."

"The boys nearby gathered excitedly end, amazed at Mukunda's courage. The bully grinned sadistically. "Gladly!" he cried, removing his hands from Bharatam. Turning toward Mukunda, he leaped at him like a hungry tiger. Lifting Mukunda high in the air, the boy dashed. the child on the ground.

As the bully bent over to raise the child high in the air again, Mukunda seized his opportunity. Quickly with both arms, he grasped the big boy around the neck, squeezing it as hard as he could. The bully, try as he would, couldn't force Mukunda to relax his hold. He beat the child's head frantically against the ground time and again, rendering him almost unconscious. Still Mukunda hung on.

"Do you give up?" Mukunda at last managed to say.

Gasping for air, the boy finally answered, "Yes, yes! I give up. Let go my throat!"

As soon as Mukunda had freed the bully, he broke faith, He leaped a second time at Mukunda. But this time all the boys around them cried, "Mukunda has beaten you fairly. If you fight him again, we'll all jump on you."

Heeding this threat, the bully grudgingly acknowledged that he had been bested.

Mukunda became a hero to his schoolmates. He had beaten a boy twice his size, to protect a friend. But later, when Mukunda was alone, his conscience gave him more pain than did his aching body. Alas! in the fight he had allowed himself to become a little wrathful. Even righteous anger was not becoming in a devotee of God, he told himself.

Raising his hand, he made a solemn vow: "Never, from this day forth, shall I allow myself to become angry."

And from that day on, never again did he know anger, no matter how deeply men sought to hurt him.

Though he could be fiery when occasion demanded, though he was forced to scold the disciples when they needed it, he never lost a divine inner calmness. Nor did he cease from loving and forgiving all the error- stricken children of earth.

A TRUE DEVOTEES ZEAL

That which characterized the youthful Mukunda more than anything else was his constant yearning for God, his practical determination to find Him. While other, much older devotees contented themselves with a little meditation and a great deal of talk, Mukunda went silently to sun-scorched places to meditate.

Often he would assume the lotus posture under the noonday sun on the hot sands in Puri.

Most people would not dare even to walk at midday on the beach; yet there Mukunda would sit for hours at a time, wrapped in divine peace. He would go into the water up to his neck and stand there chanting; hours would drift by unnoticed.

Often at night he would visit a crematory ground; what better reminder of mortal impermanency? He would sit there all night, lost in the unfathomable bliss of meditation.

In Benares he used to go to a certain temple. There he found an opening in the floor just wide enough for him to squeeze through if he went down sideways. Considering that he was only a boy, and thin for his age, it must have been small indeed.

The opening led to a series of steps; three flights down he would go. Though all was darkness he could take no candle with him, because of the lack of fresh air. He had discovered a little niche, just big enough to sit in.

Beyond the earthly silence, the supernal Aum sound would be loudly booming in his inward ear. He would practice the Kriya Yoga technique* once or twice, and pass quickly into a state of divine ecstasy.

*In his childhood Mukunda was initiated into Kriya Yoga by his father, a direct disciple of Lahiri Mahasaya. In 1910, at the age of seventeen, Mukunda met the great Kriya Yogi, "his beloved Guru Sri Yukteswarji.

Another favorite place of meditation was a little attic room in his family home at 4 Gurpar Road in Calcutta.

Many a sacred hour he spent in that room, robed in a mantle of shining peace, fervently reminding the Divine Mother of his love for Her, calling Her to come to him, Many times She came, too, touching him with Her wand of ecstasy.

One evening he came home wearily. He had worked extremely hard that day, cooking for and serving hundreds of poor people. His body couldn't have felt less inclined to sit even for a few minutes in meditation. Exhausted, he fell into bed.

"This is one night," he thought, "when I shall sleep without first meditating. I have been working hard for God all day. There is surely enough merit in that."

"But his meditative habits scolded him.

"Don't bother me!" the youth exclaimed, fighting his own conscience. "Let me rest." Ah, sweet sleep! what better reward for such a strenuous day—and a day spent in service to Divine Mother, after all? Wasn't that excuse enough?

But his conscience would not relent. "Forget your aches and pains! What about God? Doesn't your heart ache after Him any more?"

A voice (a manifestation of the cosmic delusive force) was suddenly audible in the room.

It said, as though in answer to Mukunda's conscience: "Poor boy! He will catch his death of cold! Poor boy! He has worked hard and is so tired! Let him sleep!"

Disdainfully Mukunda flung the blankets to the floor, sat upright, and locked his body in the lotus posture, Fixing his mind firmly on God, he began to meditate. Five, fifteen, thirty minutes passed. His weary body cried that surely by now he had done his duty.

"I will not sleep," Mukunda vowed with adamant determination, "until I have felt the presence of Divine Mother."

Suddenly Her ineffable ecstasy overwhelmed him. Bathed in a sea of light and joy, he spent the remainder of the night awake in God. At dawn he felt a refreshment beyond any that a night's long sleep could bestow.

Divine Mother had renewed his strength; his body ached no more. Filled with gratitude, he went forth to serve Her yet another day.

GOD IS IN EVERYTHING

There is a certain sect in India that teaches its adherents to make one mixture of all the food they are going to eat at a meal. These heroic devotees soon learn to overcome attachment to the sense of taste.

Mukunda, hearing of this practice, decided to try it. For a few days it gave him strange sensations. Mixing salt and sugar, vegetables and dessert produced an unsavory dish, But after a little while Mukunda realized that he had lost all trace of greed for food. Having thus gained complete control over his palate, he ate normally again.

But one day he did something drastic. Walking along a street with Surendra, a young friend, Mukunda noticed a large mass of decaying rice on the pavement ahead.

The stench of the rice, perceptible even from a distance, had attracted swarms of flies. But Mukunda assured himself, “God is in everything.”

At that moment a cow approached, smelled the rice, and backed away. Mukunda smiled. “Well, the cow is ignorant,” he thought. “She doesn’t see God there.” Aloud, he said, “I can eat that rice.”

Surendra laughed derisively. “If you do, I also will eat it!”

Mukunda chuckled. “All right! Remember your promise.” Without hesitation he scooped up a big handful of rice, brushed off the flies, and with relish began to eat the putrid grain.

Surendra, aghast, fled for his life. But Mukunda took another big handful of rice and raced after Surendra.

Catching him, Mukunda stuffed the slimy rice into his mouth. It was too much for his friend.

He lost everything that he had eaten for some time, Later, smiling ruefully, he said, “In the future, when I'm with you, I'll watch my words!”

Mukunda suffered no ill effects, He was happy in the realization that God's light, manifesting as the body of Mukunda, had but absorbed another portion of God's light, manifesting as the handful of rotten rice. **Could God hurt God?**

"GHOSTS" TO THE RESCUE

One night Mukunda's neighborhood in Calcutta was disturbed by a noisy sankirtan (group singing). Alternating the drums and the bells, the singers continued hour after hour to shatter the nocturnal peace.

Into their songs the men infused none of the softness of love that draws a divine response. Drunk, rather, with the love of noise, the singers seemed bent on gaining a heavenly interview by force.

The stillness-loving dawn was appearing timidly ere the men, hoarse from nightlong exertion, ended the tumult. Unfortunately for the neighbors it was almost time for them to get up and meet their daily duties. A leaden-eyed community faced the morning sun that day.

A delegation from the neighborhood sought out the house in which the sankirtan of the night before had taken place. The men there proved to be a group of rather simple-minded, superstitious people. They were apparently lacking in regard for the feelings of others. They themselves had enjoyed the music; they could not understand why outsiders had been offended.

"You mind your business, and we'll mind ours," said one of them, shrugging his shoulders as if to imply that only an unholy curiosity could have kept the neighbors awake all night. 'With keen anticipation he began to finger his Mridanga (drum).

"Besides," argued another, "a little noise—not that we make any, mind you—but still, a tiny bit of noise is good, especially at night. It keeps ghosts and demons away." The others in the group nodded their heads in earnest assent.

The nights of the following week brought little sleep to the harrowed neighborhood.

One day a man lamented, “The uproar of those fellows is enough to wake the dead.” Mukunda, over hearing the remark, suddenly smiled. Turning to a friend, he said, “That's it! That's how we'll stop them.”

“What do you mean?” asked his friend.

“A plan about the ghost-fearing devotees,” answered Mukunda, laughing. “Let us get a group of boys together. Tell each one to bring a tin pan and a large kitchen spoon. We'll meet in my house tonight at ten o'clock.”

Among his playmates Mukunda was well known for mischief and hilarious pranks. He had no difficulty in gathering a large band of boys to participate in his latest scheme.

Though as yet he had given them no more than a hint of his plans for the evening, smiles of anticipatory delight, ill concealed from the observing eyes of teachers and parents, danced on their faces for the remainder of the day.

By the time the boys had assembled that night, the neighborhood song-fest was already in full sway. Mukunda came with a box of firecrackers in his hands.

After he had confided his plan to the boys, they crept stealthily near the house in which the sleep shattering festival was being held.

Caution was scarcely necessary in all that din; nevertheless, lest their plans go awry, they took pains to move quietly as they stationed themselves in a dark place near the open windows.

Within, the singers could be dimly seen, sitting in a circle. They were swaying back and forth.

Shouts alternated with blows on an assortment of drums, bells, and other instruments. The sounds rushed out discordantly and engulfed the night.

Suddenly, amidst the bedlam, a new noise intruded itself. Beating tin pans and emitting sepulchral moans and howls, the boys had joined the chorus.

The singers stopped, astonished. Immediately the boys followed suit. A welcome silence reigned for a moment.

“Wh-who's there?” queried one of the men, timorously. There were sounds of fearful whispering and of shifting about within the room.

“Go and see what it is,” someone said in a trembling whisper. But, understandably, no one seemed willing to obey. At last the front door was hesitantly opened.

From within, someone called out in a quailing voice, “Brother Ghost?”

It was at this moment that Mukunda threw the lighted firecrackers into the center of the room.

The ensuing explosions were accompanied by another outburst from the boys (well hidden from the view of the men inside the house), who renewed their moans and the banging of tin pans.

The singers fled. In a few minutes they were out of calling distance. The house remained untenanted for the rest of the night.

The episode was too hilarious to be kept a secret. Before the next day was over, the chagrined singers had learned from several gloating neighbors the identity of the chief “ghost.”

The angry men visited the school principal's office and demanded Mukunda’s expulsion from the school. “But surely,” the principal objected, “you must have done something to goad him to such a deed.”

"No, no,” they protested earnestly, “nothing at all. Oh, it’s true, we were singing a little every evening, but we were always finished by ten o'clock.”

“How late?” demanded Mukunda, who was present.

“Oh, perhaps occasionally a little closer to eleven that is, maybe sometimes even twelve.”

“Never later?” inquired the principal, suspicious by this time,

“Well,” they admitted reluctantly, “sometimes even till two or three, or perhaps slightly later—oh, but ever so rarely,” they insisted. “We were nearly always finished by three-thirty or four.”

“That's enough,” said the principal sternly. “If ever again I hear that you are disturbing the neighbors at such hours, I shall make it my business to teach you a lesson myself.”

The men, grinning sheepishly, agreed to discontinue the singing. They thought, perhaps, that although nightly noise might have banished true ghosts, it had summoned “ghosts” equally unwelcome.

Neighbors heard no more disconcerting “concerts.”

THE WARRIOR

The devotee who walks with God is not only gentle, like a flower; he is also strong and enduring, like an oak. Mukunda's heart could melt in tenderness at the thought of the Divine Mother; it could also be inflexible for the right, as became a bold leader and warrior.

He used his power of leadership to guide countless devotees to the path toward God; he employed his warlike valor to slay the demon of ignorance—first in himself and then in those who had asked his help in attaining the Divine.

His intrepidity was demonstrated in a difficult situation that arose in his early teens.

His family had moved to a new city. The children of the neighborhood were wild and coarse. Mukunda, whose soul was wrapped in blissful visions, felt little outer kinship with the new boys. He spent most of his time by himself.

One day he went out into the sunshine to meditate. It had been raining for several days. Now the sun, in fury, had burned away the clouds that had been hiding it; the countryside was scorched, the tall grass withered. The branches hung on the trees, too tired to sway with the wind. Or was the wind too tired to blow?

For fatigue was everywhere. The animals lowered their heads and sought shelter near the ponds, or lay in the streams to let the water lap their bodies, or dozed in the shade of trees, too weary to move. Few men ventured outdoors. But young Mukunda, his heart on God, went for meditation into a sunlit spot.

"The sun is my brother," he thought. "Its fire is needed to keep the earth alive. And I need the fire of self-control to keep alive my constant devotion to the Lord."

Seating himself on a sun-baked rock, he remained there all day, protected by God's presence. Oblivious of the sun's fire, he was wrapped in flames of divine ardor.

At nightfall Mukunda rose and started home. He crossed a field; save for a cow bestirring herself languidly to chew the grass, the field was empty.

Exulting in God's nearness, Mukunda drank in the solitude. Suddenly he saw coming toward him a group of about fifteen boys. Wrath was in their eyes.

“We've caught you at last!” they cried as they neared him.

“So you think you're too good for us, do you? Now we'll see who's too good! Sissy! Coward!”

“You call me a coward?” Mukunda said disdainfully. “There are fifteen of you.”

“Yes, fifteen,” they shouted, “and we can kill you if we like.” Their leader pushed Mukunda roughly.

Mukunda backed against a tree. Fire leaped into his eyes. “Right!” he thundered, “you can kill me.

But who among you will be the first to try it?” He glowered at them fiercely, like the scorching sun.

There was a pause. Falteringly the leader answered him at last, “We spoke in jest, Mukunda. You know we didn’t mean what we said.”

Mukunda relented then; no scorn remained in his voice as he replied, “If you want to be friends, then friends let us be.”

"Let us be friends," they answered. As Mukunda walked toward home with them, the fire in his eyes was replaced by kindliness. But that fire was in his bosom nonetheless—a flame that later spread a message of truth across the world.

(Once an American student of Paramahansaji's, hearing this story, asked, "Master, would you have hurt any of those boys?"

Paramahansaji chuckled. "I knew it would not come to that," he replied. "But even a person of non-violence has a right to a warning hiss!")

THE YOUTHFUL GURU

Wherever he went, Mukunda was always surrounded by friends. Sometimes his father would give him and his companion, passes on the train to some distant city; Mukunda would hardly have descended from the train before he would be surrounded by a group of boys.

As bees are attracted to a flower, so strangers were drawn to the young Bengali, they knew not why.

Mukunda was a savior of souls, even as a child.

One morning, in school, he heard God speaking to him. In obedience to the divine command, Mukunda wrote a note to the boy sitting next to him in the class-room; it read: "I am your Guru."*

*A Guru is one ordained by God to guide other devotees back to conscious oneness with Him.

The classmate read the note and then shook his head in disbelief.

That night the classmate had a vision. The Lord showed him the truth of that which he had doubted in the morning at school.

His heart was thrilled to know that he had indeed found his Guru. On the next day he sought Mukunda eagerly.

But little Mukunda hid from him playfully. In his omniscient soul he knew all that had happened. His friend hunted for his youthful Guru, but to no avail. It was hours before he found Mukunda.

Similar is the soul's romance with God. He often comes to us; alas for our own welfare! we ignore Him.

When the dawn of understanding rises on our darkened souls, we run after Him with our heart's devotion. But God becomes playful then; He hides from us who had earlier rejected Him.

Ah, but if we are persistent, will the Lord conceal Himself for very long? The saints tell us that He cannot resist the cries of a single-hearted devotee.

KRISHNA COMES !

Sixteen-year-old Mukunda rose tranquilly from his early morning worship in the garden and went toward the Ganges to bathe. As he walked, tears of love for all God's creation came into his eyes. He glanced up. How majestic was the sun as it first appeared in the heavens!

How softly ran the clouds over the blue sky, like maiden messengers of a heavenly peace! Mukunda smiled, watching the grass nod and wave before the breeze as if it, too, was thrilled with God's love. Glad carols leaped from the throats of birds; Mukunda's footsteps lightened as he walked.

Hearing the song- birds, watching the rhythmical dance of all Nature, he felt that his heart would burst for very joy. He began singing of love for the Lord. The morning air rang with the devotional music. Soon he reached the river Ganges and, still singing, bathed in the water.

Wasn't God very near that day? The dance of His lotus feet of love seemed audible. Life, death, health, disease, pleasure, pain before Mukunda's enraptured gaze these shadows melted and were no more. Only one Ocean of light shone blissfully.

In that Ocean he saw everything dwelling, like little waves that dance and change and disappear on the surface of the sea. All Life is one. To Mukunda nought was, except that Life — a Life that breathed with joy in every atom of creation.

Hours passed. Mukunda remained in the water, as though transfixed. His voice carried far across the Ganges, leaping over the waves, He sang of his devotion to God; he sang of his deathless trust. Ere his tears of love touched the water, they became transmuted into divine jewels of joy.

When at last, continuing his chanting, he left the Ganges, the sun had already changed its course in the heavens. Like an arrow shot from a bow, rising unerringly, it had tired at last.

Gracefully now it dipped its head as though hunting a resting place in the earth below. Mukunda was so engrossed in the Lord that he was unaware of his own self. He had forgotten the customs of man, (Was he not far more than man today? He was the secret Life that danced in every leaf, that nodded and smiled in every flower.)

Drunk with the thought of God, he bad neglected even to dress himself in his dhoti-cloth when he had come out of the water.

Oblivious of everything but the Divine, he strolled chanting through the streets. Though he was without clothing, no one, strangely, seemed concerned.

He had walked for about ten minutes when an aunt of his spied him. Aghast, she approached him swiftly, saying, “Evil creature! What are you doing, passing through the streets like that?”

“Evil?” he asked, not knowing what she meant, scarcely recollecting who she was.

“Wicked boy!” she shouted. “Look at you! Just look at you! Where are your clothes? How dare you walk about like that and disgrace your father’s good name?”

Mortal memory then returned to Mukunda: he was offending some worldly custom; his dhoti had been left by the riverbank. Smiling calmly, he gazed at his aunt. “The sin is in you,” he replied.

She struck him angrily. Mukunda turned away and, singing, went back to the Ganges to retrieve his dhoti.

When he left the riverbank a second time, he was wearing his dhoti. A young friend, Bivhuti, accosted him.

“Mukunda!” his friend cried, laughing, “I saw you before, walking about like a young Adam. What on earth possessed you?”

Mukunda smiled. “God! God possessed me. And He still possesses me.”

“God!” his friend cried, a suggestion of a jibe in his voice. “Always God! If God comes to-men, why can’t I see Him? Why can’t my mother see Him? She meditates all the time. Why is the world full of people who keep calling Him, but who never see Him?”

Mukunda’s eyes were deep and still. "They never see Him because they never try to see Him.”

‘Never try!” the other exclaimed.

“Never sincerely try, I mean.” Mukunda’s smile was remote from this world. “Isn't He a Lord of love? He longs to appear openly to His devotees.”

“If He longs to, then why doesn’t He do so?” his friend inquired.

“Because He can find no room in cluttered hearts that yearn for worldly things. Devotees must want Him, and only Him. As the drunkard craves wine, so must the devotee crave the nectar of God's love.”

Bivhuti, somewhat swayed by Mukunda's eloquence, was still doubtful. "Well, perhaps someday—in the next life, or..." He smiled as if to say "never."

"Why later? Why not now?' Mukunda demanded. His voice was positive. "When devotees have learned to say with utter faith, 'Today! Today I must see Thee, Lord!'—then He will come. Why should He hide any more?"

'Bivhuti's gaze was thoughtful. "Do you mean that if we sat down this very night, and really called to - Him, He would come?"

"Why should He refuse us—we who don't refuse Him?" the young yogi said softly.

Enthusiasm came into Bivhuti's eyes. "And why should He hide from us, if we hide nothing of ourselves from Him?"

Mukunda smiled happily. "He does not keep us in darkness when we long for His light!" Gratitude for countless divine favors rang in his voice.

"Tonight! Why not tonight?" his friend said. "We'll go to your room and call Him and call Him until He can't hide any more."

"Agreed!"

"We'll stay all night!" Bivhuti vowed.

The friends parted, their hearts glad with anticipation.

The sun had set. The stars were beginning to show themselves like small shy children, hesitantly peering from behind the skirts of gathering night.

The two young boys went to the small attic room in Mukunda's house. Eagerly they closed the door behind them, placed mats on the floor, and seated themselves in lotus posture.

"Do you think we might see the Lord in the form of Sri Krishna?" Bivhuti asked.

"Why not?" Mukunda replied. "Sri Krishna will surely come tonight."

"Tonight! Tonight!" his friend repeated, wonderstruck at the newborn faith in his heart.

Mukunda and Bivhuti began to chant, their faces suffused with peace. Thoughts of the world, of the day's events, of people seen, of things done, vanished from their minds. Chanting done, the boys sat straighter still. Calmly they practiced pranayama* meditation.

*Scientific methods of controlling the life force by certain breath techniques.

Earnestly, with ever growing longing, they besought the Lord as Sri Krishna to appear before them.

The stars came out of hiding, danced quietly for a time, then fled before the rising moon. One by one they reached a safe haven, hiding behind the housetops. The people of Calcutta, one by. one, sought rest in sleep. Hours passed; still the young boys sat, their hearts fixed on Krishna, Lord of Hindustan.

(Many centuries before, Sri Krishna had walked the earth. As a young boy he had played his flute by the backs of the river Jumna. The boys and maidens in the village in Gokhul, tending their cattle, would hear his music.

Hearts enraptured, they would search for him, wandering fruitlessly ever farther through the forest—until -at last they stopped, and sat still, seeking him only within the depths of their own souls. There they heard his flute notes calling gently, thrilling their souls with inner ecstasy. For Krishna came on earth to symbolize the call of the Divine Cowherd, ever luring the lost calves back to His fields of eternal joy.)

"Softly, Mukunda sang again of his love for Sri Krishna. Bivhuti joined him, his eyes filled with tears. Chanting, then meditating, then chanting again, the two boys passed the night. It was almost dawn before Bivhuti said hesitantly, "Mukunda, Sri Krishna hasn't come. I don't believe he will come now."

"He will come!" Mukunda replied. "Sit still; keep trying."

They meditated for 'another hour. Bivhuti at last sighed, "What chance is there? The dawn is breaking. Let us go to bed."

"You may go to bed, if you like. But if I die trying, I shall sit here till he comes." Mukunda spoke calmly but with iron determination.

Suddenly, within the inner temple of his being, he beheld a 'wondrous vision:; Krishna! Krishna, walking on soft clouds of gold! Krishna, thrilling the air of heaven with the music of his flute! Krishna, sweetly smiling his smile of peace! Krishna, his lotus eyes full-blown with love, softer than flowers, dispelling the darkness of night!

"I see him!" Mukunda cried. "I see him, the fair Moon of Gokhul!"

“It can’t be true. You must be imagining it,” his friend replied, his voice yet betraying a renewed note of hope.

“You shall see him yourself.” Mukunda struck his friend gently on the chest.*

(*A yogic power possessed by great devotees, whereby they can transmit to others, by a bodily touch, glimpses of divine realization.)

“I see him, too!” Bivhuti cried at once. “I see him, too!”

What bliss welled up in their hearts! Gratefully they thanked the Lord for his wondrous visitation. Bivhuti's gratitude was mixed with tears for having doubted the divine loving-kindness.

Mukunda wept for joy. “O Krishna,” he cried, “Lord of Hindustan! I have sorrowed by the lonely Jumna riverbank, where thy flute notes thrilled the air and led the wandering calves to their homes.

O Divine Krishna, lead all thy lost children, as thou hast led me, back to thy realm of everlasting bliss!”

THE WAVE AND THE OCEAN

Even as a child Mukunda had the wisdom of a sage. Many times, in his search for a guru, he would visit some noted teacher. He would often be disappointed, finding that the teacher sought, rather than bestowed, wisdom.

One day, while he was still in his teens, he heard of a holy man who was regarded by his disciples as God incarnate. Mukunda went reverently to visit him.

The teacher, however, was not so holy as his disciples liked to believe. Their flattery had gone somewhat to his head. Seeing Mukunda's humility, the man sought to impress him further. In thundering tones he declared: "I am God!"

Mukunda was repelled by the teacher's manner. "You don't say so!" the youth said with a smile.

A dark flush appeared over the man's face; wrath distorted his features.

Mukunda produced a small mirror, Holding it in front of the teacher's angry face, he said, "Look at that! Do you call that God? It is not the God I am seeking." He turned on his heel and strode out of the room,

"Stop! Stop!" the man cried. "Wait a minute!"

He ran after Mukunda, knelt before him. "I want to thank you," he said. "I am grateful; you have awakened me from a deep delusion."

Mukunda smiled at him warmly. "You are a great soul, or you would not have taken censure so humbly.

But," he continued, reproachfully, "you should never again say that you are God.

The wave cannot say it is the ocean. The ocean has become the wave. We are all little waves, dancing in the ocean of God's light.

Can anyone confine God in a little body and ego? The Lord is everywhere. Never again claim that you are God: Say, rather, that God is in you: Then you will be speaking truth."

FORTY-EIGHT HOURS IN ETERNITY

Seven and eight hours at a time though Mukunda often meditated, he would nevertheless tell himself that some day he would have a really long meditation. What indeed were seven or eight hours out of a twenty-four-hour day? Didn't men work that long daily merely to supply their material needs?

One morning as Mukunda awoke he thought, "A whole year has passed! Think, all this time I have been promising myself a long meditation. Will it always be 'tomorrow'?

Resolution leaped into his eyes. Schoolwork, the little errands and assignments of daily life, things he had planned to do—all these flitted before his mind's eye to divert him and to weaken his spiritual purpose. He banished them. "Why not today?" he asked himself, "this very morning?"

Inflexible in this determination, he climbed the stairs to his little attic room. There he seated himself in the lotus posture. He practiced Kriya Yoga, then called the Lord's name repeatedly in an inward chant that rose from the depths of his heart.

A shining memory suddenly dawned on the inner kingdom of his soul—a clear realization that he was an ever expanding ray of God's eternal light! A prodigal son no longer, he found the heavenly glory that is man's inalienable heritage.

Two days and two nights passed: forty-eight hours. To Mukunda they seemed scarcely forty-eight minutes. During the ecstatic period, his body, rendered weightless by Infinity, had risen from the floor in levitation.

(On many later occasions in Mukunda's life his soul was so lifted up in God that his very body defied the laws of gravitation.)

It was even thus, centuries ago in Spain, that the elevated figure of St.Teresa of Avila had been observed by astounded bystanders.

It was a reluctant boy who left the attic room and the divine silence to return to the pandemonium of man's bustling world. The sound of servants at their household chores, the voices of the family in rooms below, the hubbub of people and traffic in the streets outside—all struck discordantly on his ear, yet were powerless to disturb his seraphic inner peace.

As he descended the stairs his body was still so light that his feet hardly touched the steps. In the hall he met the cook, who had been suffering for many years with a pain in his spine. Mukunda touched him. The man was instantly healed. Incoherent with joy, he ejaculated words of gratitude.

It was lunch time. Mukunda joined his relatives, who, in the Indian fashion, had seated themselves on mats on the dining-patio floor.

The family* had not paid much attention to his two-day absence; on previous occasions, also, he had disappeared from their sight for one or two days. They knew that he was in the habit of going for yoga practice to the eerie crematory grounds adjoining the Calcutta bathing ghats.

*Mukunda's mother had died in 1904, when he was eleven. This beautiful incident of forty-eight hours in eternity occurred during Mukunda's high-school years.

As Mukunda ate his meal he was conscious of a transcendent detachment. His vibrant body, the forms of the people in the room what more were these than fleeting dream-pictures in the inexhaustible mind of God?

How could he ever have considered them to be enduring realities?

Looking up, Mukunda noticed that his sister-in-law was watching him with curiosity. "I'll have a little fun with the family," he decided.

Centering his consciousness in the omniscient spiritual eye, and then employing an advanced technique, Mukunda passed into a certain yogic state, one that brings to a standstill in the human body all automatic activities—heartbeat, circulation of the blood, and so on—but that does not render the yogi insensible of the external world.

Instantly Mukunda's body fell backward to the floor. His sister in-law, whose eyes had remained fixed on him, and who was nearby, uttered a frightened cry. Quickly she felt for his pulse. It had stopped. In terror the rest of the family surrounded the boy's inert form. One of them gasped, "This is what comes of practicing yoga!"

A doctor, frantically summoned, ordered that Mukunda's body be carried to a couch. After a long and painstaking examination, the physician solemnly pronounced the boy dead.

What woe invaded that household! With sobs each relative spoke praise of the boy who they believed had forever fled this earth.

In the room was a maidservant, one who used to complain about extra work whenever Mukunda would bring home his young friends. She would insult them to their faces.

Afterward she would engage in hot arguments with Mukunda over what she considered his disarrangement of the daily routine of the household.

Nevertheless there was love between them. Mukunda always called her “Maid Ma,” as she had devotedly served the family after the mother’s death.

Maid-Ma now said, “He was so mischievous! But in spite of that he was a good boy.”

After a few moments she moaned disconsolately, “O dear God! I won't have anyone to fight with any more!”

The youngster could contain himself no longer. Convulsed with merriment, he cried, “O yes, you will”

“You!” shouted Maid-Ma. “I knew you were only playing!” She seized a stick and threw it violently in his direction.

The doctor’s face was a study in amazement. This “resurrection” was a matter hopelessly beyond his professional comprehension.

The family scolded their little prankster. It was with mock severity, however; they were too deeply relieved to be really vexed.

To paraphrase Maid-Ma, Mukunda was indeed good —but he did take pleasure in occasional mischief !

DIVINE MOTHER'S MOTORCYCLE

Sometime after Mukunda had been graduated from high school, his father bought him a motorcycle with a sidecar. Mukunda used to ride in it with his master, Swami Sri Yukteswarji.

On many days they would go riding through the city, laughing merrily as the breeze filled their clothing, making it flap around their bodies as though with a kindred enthusiasm.

Mukunda was indeed pleased with his motorcycle; it was one of the most delightful things he had ever owned. One day he parked it on the street in front of his home. Later, leaving the house, he saw a man, a casual acquaintance, gazing at the vehicle admiringly.

Mukunda smiled. “Isn't it a beautiful motorcycle?”

“Oh, yes,” the man replied warmly. “If only I could have one like it!”

“Take it, then. It’s yours.”

“But—but . . . ” the man faltered, “for how much?”

“No, take it. I'm giving it to you.” Mukunda looked at him kindly.

“Do you mean it?” The man was incredulous.

“How can anyone give away such a valuable thing?”

“Of course I mean it. I couldn't enjoy it any more, knowing that you want it. I shall be much pleased if you will accept it.”

He added, “Just wait a minute, I'll get you the pink slip of ownership.” He re-entered his home and soon returned with the pink slip.

The man hardly knew how to express his gratitude.

His eyes bore eloquent testimony, however, to his heart's feeling.

Mukunda felt a divine content. “I own nothing, beloved Mother Divine,” he thought happily.

“All these things You have lent me for my use. But they belong to You, and so I give them freely to You when I see You wanting them through the hearts of others.”

"THIS BODY BELONGS TO GOD"

Mukunda was a true renunciate, even as a child. His mother's training deepened his own inclination to give his heart only to God. Once, when he was about six years old, his mother saw him talking with a little girl.

"Come away, Mukunda," she said. Her son understood that she wanted him to mix only with little boys, and willingly obeyed-her.

Such is the training in many spiritually governed families in India. For those who later choose the path of marriage, that early discipline tends to lead to happy partnerships—unions based on mutual respect and spiritual love rather than on wrong familiarity and physical passion.

It was indicated in Mukunda's horoscope, his family astrologer told him, that he would be married three times (being twice a widower). How many men accept supinely the dictates of their karma!

But Mukunda thought, "I am the soul, ever free. Why should I consider myself to be helplessly ruled by the stars? Weren't the stars made by God? He is my sole Desire. This life I give to Him alone."

It is true that on three occasions his father sought to arrange Mukunda's betrothal. Each time the young man refused to agree.

The third time, after he had been introduced to the girl whom his father wished him to marry, he heard a voice (a manifestation of the universal delusive force*) saying: "The girl is beautiful, isn't she? Why not marry her?"

“My heart is given to the Cosmic Mother!” Mukunda answered warmly. Immediately Her divine form appeared in unparalleled loveliness before him. Bestowing a tender smile, She vanished.

*“Maya or cosmic delusion is the principle of duality or oppositional states by which the fleeting phenomenal worlds arise, appearing as separate from the Immutable and Indivisible,” Paramahansaji wrote, The Old Testament prophets called Maya by the name of Satan, “the adversary.”

Another vision followed: that of a girl's body in which the internal structure was exposed to view. Blood vessels, sinews, bones! what mortal is beautiful under the skin? Laughing inwardly, Mukunda said fervently in his heart:

“Divine Mother, I want to gaze and gaze only on Your ethereal undying beauty!”

When Mukunda announced with unmistakable finality that he was never going to marry, his relatives expressed great disappointment.

But Mukunda explained, "My path is that of renunciation.” He added laughingly, “The only reason you all are taken aback is that you are sorry to be cheated out of a feast.”

(In many Indian homes the guests are sumptuously fed at weddings.)

“But don’t grieve,” he said, “there will be a marriage in the family, after all.”

Mukunda then spoke to a cousin of whom he was very fond, Prabhas Chandra Ghose. The cousin was happy to marry such a beautiful girl.

Later Prabhas accepted the same executive position in the Bengal-Nagpur Railway that Mukunda's father had wanted to give to his son.* Mukunda's destiny lay elsewhere on the path of spiritual service to all mankind.

*Prabhas Chandra Ghose served for many years as Deputy Comptroller of Stores in the Bengal-Nagpur Railway. He is vice president of Yogoda Sat-Sanga Society (founded in India in 1918 by Paramahansa Yogananda)

Sometime later Mukunda had a vision in which apparently he was a married man.* He Saw himself lying in bed, his wife beside him. Horrified, he leaped from the bed. Loudly he cried, "You gave this body to God. How dare you forget it?" Seizing a sword, he began to cut himself to pieces, bit by bit.

*A playful test of the Lord. By heart - searching visions, saints of all lands and times have been similarly tested.

On that dramatic note the vision ended. Mukunda awoke to find that he was hitting himself on the arm with the edge of his hand. There was no one beside him; he was alone, sitting on his small cot. Smiling with relief, he touched himself on the arm and said in utter joy : **"This body belongs to God."**

These lines (in “Whispers From Eternity”) are based on an experience in the Master's childhood.

“Hello, Playmate, I am Here!”

BY PARAMAHANSA YOGANANDA

Alone I roamed the ocean shore,
And saw

The wrestling waves in brawling roar,
Expressing Thine own restless life—
Thine angry mood in ripply quiver.
The violent vastness made me shiver
And turn away from Nature's strife.

And then
A spreading sentinel tree
Waved friendly arms to comfort me,
‘With gentle look sublime.
Its swaying leaves in lull'by thyme
A message sang I knew was Thine.

Above
I scanned the gaugeless sky;
Within its bosom dim
I childlike tried on Thee to spy,
In play with Thee.

In vain I sought Thy body, hiding nigh,
Cloud-veiled, foam-sprayed, leaf-garlanded,
Too fine mine eyes to see;
Thy voice too pure mine ears to heat.
And yet

I knew that Thou wert always near,
At hide-and-seek with me;
Receding, Spirit Dear,
When almost I had touched the robe of Thee.

I groped for Thee through fold on fold
Of ignorance old, as time is old.

At last
My search I stopped in dull despair,
My search for Thee, O Royal Sly Eluder!
. . everywhere,
Yet seeming nowhere . . . lost in unplumbed space,
Where none may clasp Thee nor behold Thy face,

In haste,
I hied away from Thee.

Still, still no answer from the rageful sea,
And whispers only from the kindly tree;
Just silence from infinitudes of sky,
From valleys low and mountains high.
Hurt child, within the depths of me
I hid and sulked, not seeking Thee.

When lo!
Unheralded, an Unseen Hand
Removed the maddening band
That blinded me in darkness old.
With joy untold
I turned and saw
A laughing sea, not one of wrathful roars;
A gay glad world, with open astral doors.

With only mists of dreams between,
Beside me Someone stood unseen,
And whispered to me, cool and clear:

"Hello, playmate! I am here!"

901

Other Books are also available from **Swami Yoganandaji** at Amazon, Flipkart & Pothi.com

Sr.No.	Name of the Books & Links thereof
1	Lahiri Mahasaya's 371 Guidelines to Kriya Practitioners Amazon.in - https://amzn.to/3rQx7gO Flipkart.com - https://bit.ly/3S0nXJd Pothi.com - https://bit.ly/48QYlo9
2	Biography of Yogiraj Sri Sri Shyama Charan Lahiri Mahasaya Pothi.com - https://bit.ly/3rHtrxW
3	Swami Yogananda's Super Advanced Course (Lessons 1 to 12) (1930 Original Edition) Pothi.com - https://bit.ly/3tE1kjr
4	The Cosmic Mother - One Aspect of God (1945 Original Edition) Pothi.com - https://bit.ly/45r7a5a
5	Original Teachings of Swami Yoganandaji Vol.-1 (Praecepta Step 1 to 3, Lessons 1 to 77) : Pothi.com - https://bit.ly/3tzfCCd
6	Original Teachings of Swami Yoganandaji Vol.-2 (Praecepta Step 4 to 6, Lessons 79 to 152) : Pothi.com - https://bit.ly/3ZT2805
7	Swami Yogananda's 5 Yogoda Lessons of 1925 Pothi.com - https://bit.ly/46KeGZQ

8	The Holy Science by Sri Yukteshwar Giri (1920 Original Indian Version) Pothi.com - https://bit.ly/3FinSJm
9	The Rubaaiyat of Omar Khayyam - A Spiritual Interpretation by Swami Yogananda (1937 Original Edition) Pothi.com - https://bit.ly/3LY3WPC
10	The Autobiography of a Yogi (Original & Unaltered. First Edition,1946) Pothi.com - https://bit.ly/3S9mD6j
11	Scientific Healing Affirmation (1925 Original Edition) Pothi.com - https://bit.ly/3POLpq8
12	The Original Bhagavad Gita - A Spiritual Interpretation by Swami Yogananda (1932 Original Edition) Pothi.com - https://bit.ly/3vpNgLw
13	Swami Yogananda's - Comparison of the Scriptures (1932 Original Edition) Pothi.com -
14	The Science of Religion (1920 Original Edition) Pothi.com - https://bit.ly/46utsnX
15	Whispers from Eternity (1929 Original Edition with Signature of Swami Yoganandaji) Pothi.com - https://bit.ly/46wh1YF

16	Paramhansa Yogananda's Chief Disciple Dr. Minott W. Lewis' Discourses (Volume-1) Pothi.com - https://bit.ly/3LWWuo4
17	Paramhansa Yogananda's Chief Disciple Dr. Minott W. Lewis' Discourses (Volume-2) Pothi.com - https://bit.ly/3QdwNSx
18	Atma Katha - The Authorized Story of Sri Sri Yukteshwarji's First Disciple - Shri Matital Mukhopadhyay Pothi.com - https://bit.ly/3ZSKjyh
19	Paramhansa Yogananda's - Metaphysical Meditations (1952 Original Edition) Pothi.com - https://bit.ly/3rTYnuU Amazon.in - https://amzn.to/3QinWiD Flipkart.com - https://bit.ly/3rTYkPK
20	Songs of the Soul (1923 Original Edition) Pothi.com - https://bit.ly/3tyZXTm
21	Original Teachings of Swami Yoganandaji Vol.-3 (All Praecepta Summaries, Lessons 1 to 182) : Pothi.com -

22	Original Teachings of Swami Yoganandaji Vol.-4 (Praecepta Step 7, Lessons 148 to 182) : Pothi.com - https://bit.ly/45zdyqS
23	Stories of Mukunda - Early life of Paramahansa Yogananda (1958 Original Edition) Amazon.in - https://amzn.to/3LXNUW3 Flipkart.com - https://bit.ly/3LWZgt9 Pothi.com - https://bit.ly/3PZGmU1
24	Life, Mission & History of Paramhansa Yogananda Pothi.com - https://bit.ly/3M16Y5C
25	Swami Yogananda's East-West Magazines (Vol.1 thru Vol.4) Pothi.com - https://bit.ly/3QiOa4D
26	Swami Yogananda's East-West Magazines (Vol.5 thru Vol.7) Pothi.com - https://bit.ly/46KeE4R
27	Swami Yogananda's East-West Magazines (Vol.8 thru Vol.9) Pothi.com - https://bit.ly/3rQBUPc
28	Swami Yogananda's East-West Magazines (Vol.10 thru Vol.12) Pothi.com - https://bit.ly/48LpDw2

29	Swami Yogananda's East-West Magazines (Vol.13 thru Vol.15) Pothi.com -
30	The Psychological Chart by Swami Yogananda (1925 Original Edition) Pothi.com - https://bit.ly/496WGtS
31	String of Gems from Autobiography of a Yogi (From 1946 Original Edition) Pothi.com - https://bit.ly/4bqEyxh
	# UPCOMING BOOKS AT AMAZON, FLIPKART & POTHI.COM :
32	The Original Second Coming of Christ - A Spiritual Interpretation by Swami Yogananda (1932 Original Edition)
33	Cook Your Food With Yogananda - Delicious Recipe Booklet (1935-1936 Original Edition)
34	Swami Yogananda's Super Cosmic Advance Course (1930 Original Edition)
35	12 Set of Yogoda Lessons by Swami Yogananda (1925 Original Edition)
36	Aumkar Gita by Lahiri Mahasaya
37	Swami Yogananda's East-West Magazines (From 1925 to 1952 in 7 Big Volumes)

Blank page for my notes :-